Autobiography

of a

Dan Brady

Volume One

One Insight Press

Copyright © 2020 Daniel Brady
All rights reserved
Printed in the United States of America
Cover and interior photos from Dan
Author photo by Clara Hsu

ISBN 13: 978-0-578-64415-8
ISBN 10: 0578644158

One Insight Press
San Francisco, CA

Please see my author's page on Amazon.com
https://www.amazon.com/author/dan-brady

Foreword!

Welcome to the portals of the past, mazes of memory, the reservoir of reflections, the quilt of quietude, the translucent wash of wonders, and profound seasons of silence.

Dan

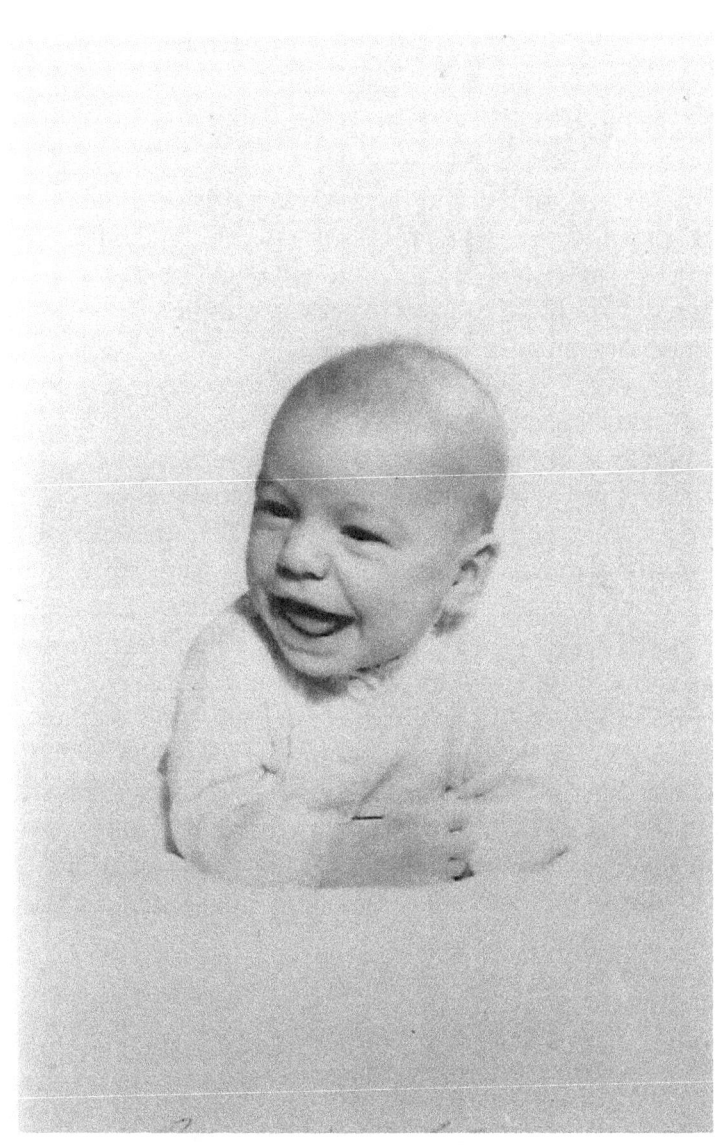

See? Here I am at three months.

Introduction:

    This autobiographical collection was partly inspired by my age, 67 this past year. The process of assembling the manuscript provided enough sadness and joy to give me a mental and emotional work out. I did notice gaps, events and circumstances important enough to be included but which I've never written about, however, I wanted to keep this simple – deciding to use only pieces I already had. The collection is organized in chapters according to periods of my life, the pieces reflecting or representing my experience. Some pieces are based on memories, some on reflections, even workshop prompts, while others, mainly those later on, were written concurrent with the events or circumstances they are meant to portray. There are some pieces appropriate to more than one section. There are poems about friends, significant events, or internal dialogues, thoughts, and revelations. You may note stylistic variations, which may be because I kept older poems formatted as they were. You may note words or phrases in parentheses; I do this to indicate the presence of homonyms I wish to reference. I've also enjoyed the luxury of including leisurely prose pieces. I hope you'll enjoy the journey, find something of use, and, as with all of my books, pass it along.

                                                          Dan

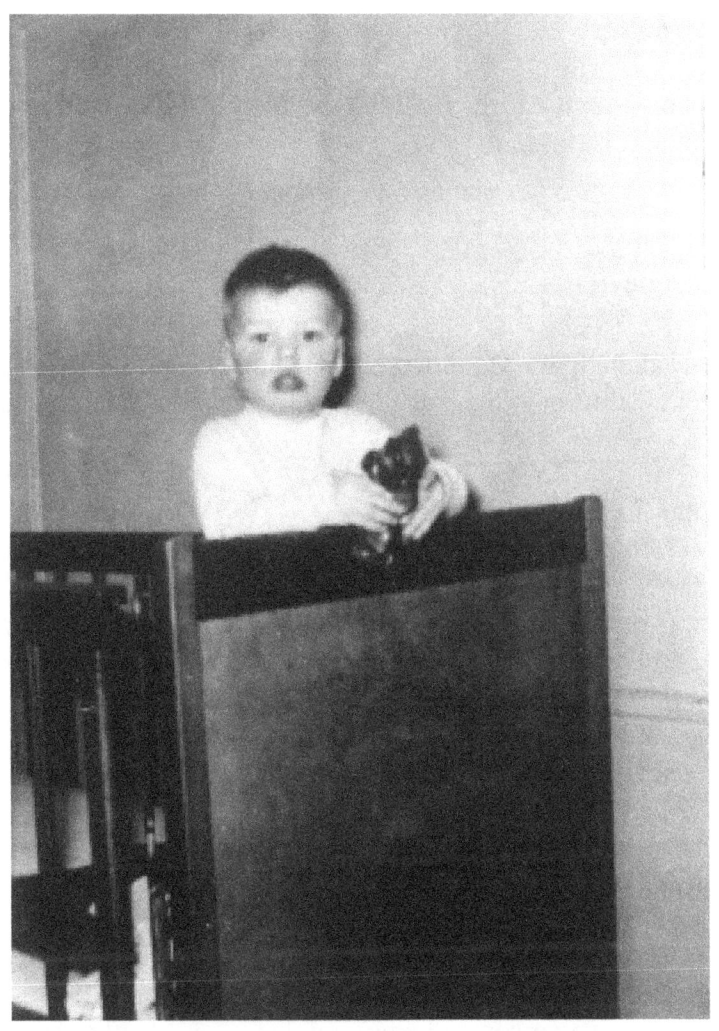

This picture is, maybe, a year or so later.

Volume One   Table of Contents

Chapter One   **1 to 55**
5/2/8 – 60/6   **New York City**

I was born August 16th, 1952 in New York City. I was the forth born of seven children.

Chapter Two   **56 to 96**
60/5 – 72/9   **Fremont**

After Dad died, my Mom moved us from New York City to Fremont California. She had been born in or near Sacramento.

Chapter Three   **97 to 126**
72/9 – 75/8   **S.F. State**

This was only a four-year stretch but it was the first time I was truly on my own working odd hours as an orderly in a facility caring for elders. I learned how to make ends meet. For a time I lived on Jules Avenue, where I first self identified as a poet. This was also when I began working full time.

Chapter Four   **127 to 139**
75/8 – 78/5   **32nd Avenue**

I continued working full time and writing. I was, for the most part, a reclusive person and enjoying quantities of solitude.

Yes! Give this book away!   **140 to 142**

In Volume Two

Chapter Five   **1 to 88**
78/5 – 89/3   **6th and Irving St.**

During this time I lived in the inner sunset of San Francisco. I became more involved with writing and learned a great deal, began to publish, attend open mics, and connect with the Theosophical Society where I established several important friendships.

1	**Friends and Family**	1 to 20
2	**Politics as Unusual**	21 to 35
3	**Metaphysics and Philosophy**	36 to 61
4	**Personal Notes**	62 to 88

Chapter Six   **89 to 136**
89/3 – 96/11   **21st Avenue**

Writing was put aside for a few years because teaching took up a great deal of time and married life became vitally important to me. By the early 90's I began going first to haiku and then open mic poetry events.

In Volume Three

Chapter Seven   **1 to 121**
97/12 – 11/8   **University St.**

I was full time teaching as Wendy and I managed the usual ups-and-downs of life, not to mention the passing of family members and friends.

1	**Relationship and Romance**	1 to 29
2	**Self Portraits**	30 to 45
3	**Passings and Life Notes**	46 to 67
4	**On Poetry, Art, and Perceptions**	68 to 89
5	**More Politics as Unusual**	90 to 121

Chapter Eight   **122 to 223**
11/8 – present   **30th Avenue**

I went to open mics, began hosting Sacred Grounds, retired from teaching, and began to publish prose and poetry.

1	**Love, Life, and Liberation**	123 to 163
2	**History, Memoirs, and Hopes**	164 to 194
3	**Considerations**	195 to 202
4	**One Thing Leads to Another**	203 to 212
5	**Insights and Visions**	213 to 223

****

Chapter One

52/8 – 60/6 New York City

I was born August 16, 1952 in New York City. I was the forth born of seven children and to my memory my childhood, for most of this time, was happy. I did have a major mishap when I fractured my right tibia, there was surgery to remove a marrow infection; this incapacitated me for a time and was life-altering in the long term. While I was hospitalized, I acquired a life long fear of hypodermic injections, and severe orthopedic consequences, which only became more pronounced as I aged. That last also presaged a series of surgeries in my teens. Becoming disabled affected my development both socially and emotionally as it influenced what I could and could not do. Still, there were many happy memories as the poems in this section illustrate. However, my life was suddenly overshadowed when, in November 1959, my Dad died of a sudden heart attack. This change prompted further effects, which became pronounced after Mom returned to California with us. She was been born in Sacramento and had relatives willing to help her resettle, ultimately, in Fremont, one of the first planned cities in the United States.

Bridget Shannon, my grandmother on my Dad's side, is seen here on the right. She is with her best friend Bella. This portrait may have been taken in Ireland.

My grandfather, John Brady, is on the roof of the Brady home at East 70th Street, New York City. John married Bridget Shannon in New York City about 1906. John was born in Cootehill, County Cavan, Ireland. Bridget Shannon was born in Killashandra, also in County Cavan, about 1881. She emigrated to New York City around 1900. Although they married there is no record as to when and where. Bridget worked as a "living out" girl, a domestic who did not live with the family. He worked as a stevedore, interior home construction, and had a try at the saloon business.

This quite formal portrait is of my grandfather, on my mother's side, Egidio Belluomini, with his second wife, Emma, taken at the Cliff House and Sutro Baths in San Francisco, 1918.

This photograph shows a young Emma Gianpaoli Belluomini, my grandmother, with my mother.

	BRADY	
1882	BRIDGET S. BRADY	1929
1918	MARY BRADY	1930
1885	JOHN BRADY	1941
1946	MARY ANN BRADY	1946
1948	NOREEN BRADY	1949
1884	BRIDGET BRADY	1965
1909	MARGARET BRADY	1990
1911	ANNA BRADY CARNEY	2001

MY JESUS MERCY

This is the family grave marker in New York City. It shows Bridget Shannon Brady, my grandmother. It was through her that I acquired Irish citizenship. I am now a dual citizen of the European Union and the United States. There are stories on this stone; Mary Ann Brady and Noreen were but toddlers before passing on. From what I understand, those born before 1905 were immigrants to this country and those born afterwards were first generation citizens.

Upon Conjuring My Ancestors

What constellations oversaw their births.
Providing the metaphysical light
By which they came into being and grew into their clans?
What stories did their elders tell
Of the sky being made just for them?
What adventures did near hills or virginal stands provide?
What secrets lay tumbled under the stonework of fallen tombs
What wishes escaped the rocky verge of vernal springs?
This speculation applies to Ireland
During the misty millennia before the invasion,
Usurpation, infamy, and famine, "The Great Theft."
Just as it applies to Tuscany
Where, beside a simple, yet beautiful lagoon,
My grandfather's hands tended earth and flora
Though he would, when he could, work near to the big house
Where Puccini composed,
Playing and pausing as inspiration dictated
Exploring the unexpected or inspired variations.
He played so wonderfully
That my grandfather, only an assistant gardener,
But avid opera fan,
Took every opportunity to be near
When the great man played.
This was one family legend.

These two family trees
Uprooted themselves for transplant to America.
Mom was born near Sacramento about 1920
And Dad, on the eastern seaboard,
In the Empire City of New York.

Dad's parents were John and Bridget –
Mom's were Emma and Egidio.
All made their way over the seas,

Managed their frugal capacities,
Working from can't see to can't see,
Went from get go to let go and
Believed in a bright future
Even though they couldn't see it.
There is little known about grandpa John.

He did finishing work on the interiors of homes,
Had a bar and was proud of it.
In one of the rare photos I have.
I recognized the Brady face.
His wife, Bridget, died in 1929, just after the crash.
Legend has it that she was a strong woman
Being more than equal to John in all things, save size.

Grandma Emma was domineering
Abusive, so I hear, while Egidio was meek,
And completely outweighed
By her strength of will, and pointed character.

They all passed on before I knew them
And are the unexplored country,
The buried foundations
Of my elusive past.
From them I do have inheritances though ...
Of height, hand, and leg
Certainly of face, and smile
Not to mention of music, song, being hopeful of heart, and
Helpful of soul.
God rest them well and
Bless us all, every one!

My mother, the middle child, is seen with two of her older cousins; Oakland's Lake Merrit is in the background.

Mom – In Four Movements

1)

When we think of her ... hidden self
The shadows of which   we hardly ever saw
Behind her disguises and camouflage
How she kept house, order, and managed schedules
Or her tears ... out of sight
Let her good sense of humor roll out long and loud
Or loose her brash, unbridled attitude at any weakness
She made the potlucks in abundance
Worked with kids – hers and everyone else's
Not visibly eccentric
A native Californian
An abused child
A widow
And sufferer of life
Who ... would give you her mind
In a mouthful
Tell you to keep a stiff upper lip
Sting your errors with but a word or glance
Or gentle you with her good right hand
She could have had another husband ... lovers certainly
Yet she did not play it that way – and now she is legend
And our weak memories belie her sheer, forceful sanity,
Her vision, and smirking attitude
Toward all but the most serious of mischief
Her language of economy and vocabulary of pain

2)

There was this one photo; she was in an unfenced backyard
Open to the countryside – with some low hills in the distance
She was standing with two other women – all young
Laughing
She remembered only one of their names
Couldn't remember where it was,
How she'd gotten there
Or exactly or when the picture was taken …
In the photo they were playing around a tree
She said they'd been throwing apples at each other
But also there seemed, a mystery
Because she paused in that brief telling
To look up … away
And became still as she … looked something over in her mind
As if to make a decision …
Before looking back to me, who was staring
And quickly added, "Oh that's about it."

3)

In another photo
She was sitting on a park bench
It was a bright day … but she was in dappled shade
This was before her marriage was even a thought
Before World War Two, New York City, children, widowhood
Before her veterans died
And her mourning for them one and all –

4)

"You know, Danny," she'd like to say, near the end of her life,
"It's not as if miracles don't happen much anymore …"

Her sweat for my fever
Her muscles for my
Diseased ... weak bones ...

July 7th, 1944: My Mom and Dad on their wedding day with Babe Paladini and Louisa Souza at Saint Vincent Ferrar's Church, New York City, New York.

A eucalyptus leaf
fell out of the X's
during my research of a science project
for my tenth grade class;
Mom said
it was from the east,
when she was young
and was dreaming about
the rolling summer brown hills in California;
she was strolling through Central Park with my father,
they shared pink popcorn, walking past the duck pond
on a blue and white day;
she said that she remembered
a little boy who pushed a boat out onto the water
and was alarmed when it did not come back to him,
so smooth,
the way it sailed,
the breeze and the ripples at its bow
how they faded away.

she was young
and the wind blush autumn
of New York City was on her face;
her heart was adrift in the clouds
through the sky
in her mind

        Inclined to glide – this
        Way or that   the hawk   above
        The Mission's brown hills

Mom is third from the left. A neighbor is holding me. This may be where we lived before 207th St.

Charley Shannon (far left) claims to have been in the bar business long than anyone else. His café near 68th Street does a brisk busine

On the left is the same Charlie Shannon who will be depicted later on. What is more New York than a bar run by a friendly Irishman along with his friends and family?

This is a photo of a tavern my Dad worked for a time. It was at East 70th and 2nd St. It may have been located in the basement of the building he lived in. He may have been making his own beverages; there was a robbery attempt as well as hints of stories and legends. That all said, the venture did not do well; perhaps Dad was over-generous and a bit easy-going.

Dad

I don't remember
Many years after
What your last words to me were
Anonymous ones no doubt
You had no reason to believe
You wouldn't wake up again
Did you?
So we never had those conversations
The talks
About life
The proverbial "birds and bees" for example
What it is to be a man
We never drank as men do
Laughed or raged
Cheered for our teams
Came to understand war
Looked at our medals
Compared wounds
Or shared tears for those dear ones
Lost to us
In those storms only mad men and Gods make

I avoided your funeral
I remember the long afternoon was cool and still
I hid to see if I would be missed
Heard the very full cars pull away
I hoped I wouldn't be forgotten
Which I was
To my regret
Which I feel sixty years later
Imagine that

I liked the way you imitated a harmonica
I collected records as you did

Stood up for others as Mom always said you would
Was proud of the way she said I imitated you
When I'd painstakingly look through bargain racks
Or keep things pin neat and symmetrically tidy
Oh you were buried and must now be mostly dust
None of your friends are alive   that I know of
None of your high school buddies

Your work pals
Your vet pals
Your childhood sweethearts
Anyone?
How would I know?

And who visits your grave now-a-days?
I will … I am planning on it … anyway
My first time …

From my experience with Tom
I do not know the language of the dead
Cannot hear from you
Though I have written, eternally yours
Over the years   and now add this note
From a far away time and place
One you may have imagined once
In an idyll day's chat
In dappled shade
Near to your childhood home
That I never saw

I speculate you may have gone into San Francisco
In your dress best for a few beers
A dinner or a night on the town
Speculate that as you passed through the Bay Area.
When young and the world at war,
You might have had the time of your life
Unaware of all that there was to come

Such as   love   when you met Mom
And then, after the war's dust settled,
Coming back to New York
Getting married
And heading our whole fandambly
As we used to call it
Dad, I speak in tongues
As Kathy said you did

Like you,
I can get folks to laugh
Cheer people up
And   one way or another

Always give love
To anyone one lucky enough to be there
At the right time
In the fount of it
That I somehow learned
Need never be turned off
And how
You always gave it away
I know
I feel it
That's another thing
We have in common
Thank you Dad

                              Dan

My father as a young man, dressed up for a day in Central Park, a Brady place to go, as it was not far from their home.

the leaves
of autumn
they are wind chimes
windows of color
under the ice
they are
warm red
or yellow
how
the snow
blankets them
for spring
when the rains carry these
boats to sea
swirling
this is a dance I always did
as a child:
My toes in the salty sand
my eyes looking out toward Europe
my Dad whistling

This is Charles Vincent Brady, in June 1959. It is the last photo of him as he died, a few months later, in November of that year.

Them Bones

What will they say   in their mute state,
These skeletal remains of mine –
Were they to be exhumed from their dark, damp hold

What secrets would show in the glare of objective light?
What would the calculating scientific eye find?

Probably this objectivist would take note
First of the knotted lump of fused bone
That was once my right ankle
The tibia would speak of infections, surgeries,
Hospitals, fever, and pain.

They'd see right away
That I couldn't have been much of an athlete
By any stretch.

They'd ponder how it was that my hip socket
With out surgical indications
Would show that I'd walked correctly, most of my life.
Despite evidence I'd have to have been splay footed –
At least as a young child.

What they couldn't know about
Was my mother calling out, "walk right, you can do it!"
And I would do just that, out of stubbornness or pride
Nor would they hear the doctors mumble
When they saw how we'd corrected my gait.
They would, in sectioning the tibia
Out of curiosity, if nothing else,
Find evidence, akin to tree rings,
Which would date and time the initializing trauma
That set the stage for a life of compensatory reaction
To my "bum leg."

They'd find the tracings of that hairline fracture
Which created a gateway
As big as the Grand Canyon
To the exploring staphylococcus I'd contracted.
But they wouldn't know I'd ignored Mom's directives,
Had gone out to play,
And play and play and play jumping again and again
Off the top step of the stoop
Until, finally, I hurt myself making a hairline gateway
As a result.

Would analysis of the bones –
Those "rings" show that it was late summer,
August in fact

Would they find evidence that I had been "the runner"
Or "the mouth" capable not only of telling anyone off
But of out pacing any bully, I wonder.

Would other experts, called in to analyze this "hard data,"
Surmise I was disappointed with a life of walking?
Or being just a spectator?

When they look at the tibia
What will they make of the re-grown center of infection?
What will they think of the surgery on the left knee
Will they guess it had been done to slow the left's growth
So the right wouldn't be all that much shorter?

What will the psychologists or sociologists make of the fact
That the legs would be different in length for all that effort
And my feet would be widely disparate in size and shape?
I wonder what these would make of the right foot
Would they wonder why I'd kept such a tortured member?
Would they speculate on its advantages and disadvantages?
Could they guess the real reason I chose to keep something
So, well, dysfunctional and ugly?

Psychologists, and social historians, might readily speculate
As to the effect such injuries would have on peer acceptance,
The status I'd have in high school,
The likelihood of my getting dates or having sex.
Certainly this analysis would include the speculation
On the consequences of being ineligible for the draft
And sociologists would ponder how this effected my beliefs
Could they be figure where I stood on the Vietnam War?

Perhaps they'd think the injury would be central to my character
Essential to understand who I was or how I interacted with others.
Perhaps some will wonder if this affected my marriageability –
They'd question if I'd ever been married
And they'd have reason,
Because the ring I would bear would be of silver,
Not gold
They'd not know it was my father's, given to me by my mother

Yes, that right leg would be rich ground for speculation
But then they'd come to my teeth
Finding the severe evidence of antibiotic staining
Historians and psychologists would ponder
How my appearance affected my acceptability
Knowing the premium a "healthy smile" had in my day
And so have evidence or express likelihood
Of my being a bit of an outcast.

As evidence they'd cite the late in life dental work
The upper front of crowns being the salient evidence
But they'd have to wonder why I'd waited so long,
There would be rich speculation – perhaps I was poor
And so had had to wait quite some time
And the fact that I'd had them done
Proved the value of appearance, even to me.
They'd not know about the "misunderstanding"
With my dentist.

Then too, from my hardened remains, they'd see
I'd had the mercury fillings removed, again, late in life,
Using medical forensics they'd see I changed my diet too
Giving up on meat as a source of protein,
They'd see, for the record, that I'd used supplements
Had periods of time where I exercised a great deal

If the exam were exhaustive
They'd certainly find the broken fingers, all small injuries
And wonder why there were so many
Why they were scattered throughout my life
Would they think that I was prone to fisticuffs?

What would a mineral profile my bones tell them?
About the air quality of New York versus San Francisco
Would some form of microanalysis
Show I had periods of second hand smoke?
That my Dad's brand of tobacco was Half and Half?

What else would they learn; what else would be evident?
I fear to speculate.
For this is enough to make one pause to consider
Just what kind of record any of us are leaving
Each and every day of our lives
We are therefore a book unto ourselves.
We record each trauma, each meal, each accident
To be sure
The saying, you are what you eat,
Has to be expanded, or amended
As our skeleton will certainly speak
Such that for most of all of us
It will be the only "tell all" novel
We'll ever write.

I Am From

I am from August, dusk and the playground of the street
From jump rope and tag, the spring of new Keds under my feet
From catching fireflies, from stickball, and hot pretzels with salt
From snow-cones and ring-o-levio and chocolate with malt

From the Big Apple when Coney Island was king
From sand lots, brick stoops and flying right off the swing
From hospitals, their antiseptic smell, and many needles' sting

I am from destiny and Ireland and learning as I go
From believing that help comes from above, you know
From cathedrals, Latin liturgy, and believing in god's love
From my father's sure hand and my Mom's Sunday glove

I am from spaghetti and potatoes, dinner with cowboy radio shows
From caroling, accordions, and Halloween in home made clothes

From dancing, even if wild and weird, to crude garage bands
From singing and poetry and playing drums with my hands

I am from the endless conditions, which can make birth your bind,
The gift of intuition and visions which released my heart and mind

From my core where harbors some pure and mysterious light
Providing me with comfort through this long contemporary night
From that comes hope – more precious than the wealth of a king
Which has my soul arise each day, hearken and take wing

From the muse of the universe which places my life on display
To all the endless moments between every heart beat

    Each breath
        Each thought
            Every day

This is my family, soon after I was born. Dad is holding me and it shows Mom, John, Tom, and Kathy.

Memories More Dear Than Air

And the sun was low but a good long while from setting
So it would be mildly warm with light enough to play by

Younger kids got out first and took up the sidewalks
With Ring-a-Rosie, Hop Scotch, and London Bridges
And Red Rover, Mother May I, or freeze tag on lawns
While Red Light – Green Light was out in the street …

Older kids came out after helping with the dishes
Girls, big and small, circled for jump rope, clapped, and chanted,
While the one in waiting lip synched the chant bobbing into step,
Her head moving as her eyes fixed on the arc of the rope
Kids with roller skates would talk some big boy
Into pulling them behind his bike to play crack the whip

Anyone who had them would try to run and jump the bounce
Out of their brand new Keds
And some drew with chalk on the sidewalk

Above it all great tree branches interwove above
Forming the columns and arches of a natural cathedral
Their distant tops shushing whispers, over our playground world
As dads on front stoops talked about everything
And the moms would join in with them laughing
We all knew everyone's calls or whistles

The big stick ball game would get underway
With disputed choice decided by "shooting" odds and evens
And you could "take it over" if you had to
And the game would go until no one could see the ball
Not even a brand new yellow Spaulding

Later, looking out the window we might laugh at cloud shapes
During the muggy, eternally long summer nights
When a bright full moon would hang just outside window
Learn that a slight motion in the curtains
Foretold a breathe of air … giggle at bed to bed whispers
Listen to crickets
Lonely night footsteps passing in by on the street below
Or trains sounding farther and farther away
And there are the memories; I remember Cracker Jacks
Bazooka Joe and cereal box tops
That ice pops with two sticks were for being shared
And swinging on swings so high until you were scared again

Oh there were family day a day at the beach
Coney Island, strolling the boardwalk
And that day we became bumper car kings
Drawing such a crowd with our antics
That the guy gave us free rides; we were good for business
There was a blue sky and in it
A whiff of warm cotton candy

In the fall there was cupping handfuls of fireflies
Piling up leaves for a pyre
Wearing new clothes on the first day of school
Saying, "Look at me ... look at me!"
Making up rules
When Kool Aid was cool
As was securing baby coach wheels
As Bill Cosby described it
Listening to the radio and celebrating snow days
When "take-overs" did solve everything
With your best friends

Spinning to get dizzy,
And water balloons were the bomb
A foot or so of snow a wonderland
Or mysterious landscape where everything was possible
A land where every old game became new

When any parent could discipline any child on the block
Feed them, ask a favor, no one thought anything about it
When being sent to the office was nothing
Compared to what happened with Mom
And, God help you, Dad   so yes, we did have fear
But it wasn't of gunshots or gangs ... drugs or predators
Bad food, bad media,
Or a whole world being tormented
And we really didn't want our parents to be angry at us

Mom was the prettiest, smartest
And could fix anything   with anything
And seemed to know it all

Any sweet dreams yet?
From this brief traipse into a time you may not know
A world of a bygone age

But such a dream is one I cannot forget
A simpler place … a childhood of a time
A world that went from radio to television
From baseball to the moon and beyond

To those of the current generation   I want to say
Enjoy each-and-every one of what will be your good old days
As long as you can and make them worthwhile
Something for your future to look back upon with love
Something that helps you become who you are
Which, ultimately, keeps faith alive
It is as important as the belief in truth
But to keep it simple:
Mean what you say … we did
We survived … we went out on a limb
Took risks few parents would tolerate these days
You have to have courage
I want to pass that along … everywhere I can
Fight for what is true and right
With humor, of course, and all due respect
Make determination necessary… persevere
Go for justice … be the good guy and do the right thing
Talk out your problems
Keep your friends close
Play hard and laugh out loud … come on
There's time yet
We can go out – the light is still just right
So we can play   sure we can … tag … you're it!

I am three and a half, before my leg issues, on our stoop at 207th St.

Christmas   holding hands
Snow melts between our fingers
Running home for soup

New York   winter day
Biting into a hot dog;
Its warm, buttery bun!

Naming Of Me

I began as
Daniel Philip Brady
Named after my father's ancient clan
For two uncles – on the Shannon side of the family
Who were priests and well respected
In both our family and the community

Named after a Biblical figure
Whose dealings with lions
Made for odd considerations
Or connections considering that my sun sign is Leo
And whose penchant for prophecy
Intersects neatly with the muse and how I give it my voice

When I was young my mother called me by my first name
If all was well … if all was certainly not
I would be called by my full name
First, middle, and then, with full emphatic blast, last

I was "Daniello Kabello My Fine Fat Fellow"
When Mom was in a bright mood
If I had gotten her to laugh … or we were celebrating

I was Danny Boy for a time
Because that song was popular when I was young
I disliked it however
For, because although I could not fathom why at the time …
I would cry uncontrollably
Whenever it came on the car's radio

Only later, as a young man, as I listened to the words,
Did I get an inkling into that mystery
But still, after all these years,
I wondered how I knew when so young

I was "high waters"
Whenever I first wore a pair of hand me down pants
Because I had to wear them up and noticeably so
Until I grew into them, that is, and when I grew out
Well, I became "Mr. Floods"

By high school there were the silly adventures and
The Misadventures Of Captain Zapp a would be super hero,
Whose "dramatic demeanor and profile"
Can still be seen in faded photos taken by Niels

There was Daniel P. "Ironfist" Brady
Either a legendary but non-existent prizefighter
Or the bizarre ruler of Bradisylvania
One of the three nations on the imaginary isle of Ozzefogva
A high school prank we pulled on no one ... ever
No matter our hats, uniforms, passports, maps, made up money
Or very secret handshakes ...

I was "Noah" for a time
When I needed a name but didn't want to give my real one.
I was surprised how it caught on
The joke lasted for months
But that's college dorm life for you

I became Mr. Brady when I landed my first job,
Got junk mail,
Was called by tele-marketers,
Or buttonholed on the street; I was this for some long time

I also became "teacher"
"Dad" or even "Mom" to my students
As I taught them
To eighth graders I was "Gnarly"
Or "Mr. B."
And, eventually,
"Bungalow Dan"

For a time, after I got married
When we considered taking and giving names
We considered combining our names so we'd each change
And so we mixed our various names into a hodgepodge
And McHolterbelles was the best of the lot
I'll never forget it, nor will Wendy
Then came the names we had for each other
And there are dozens of those
Chief among them are Bu, which is short for Huggerbu,
Which is engraved on the inner face of our wedding rings –
Even if a bit abbreviated.

I've had other names, of course,
Each of which, if described, linked,
As I've done with a precious few here,
Would make for a biography of sorts
Of memories,
Of times, places, and faces to be sure
And much, much more

And it all makes me wonder
How to respond when someone says,
"Well, what's in a name?"

The Street As Diamond

The old manhole cover was home base
Because it never moved.
Now, most days, first base was the driver's side rear door
Of Mr. Donovan's blue and white '55 Buick.
Of course, second changed up a lot
Sometimes it was a chalk drawn square, when we had chalk.
Once, for a whole season,
It was a ruined blue and white washcloth.
However, most often, it was a random piece of cardboard,
Which we'd sprinkle with water and stomp down into place.
Usually, by the top of the third, it was definitely fixed –
Which was good.
Third, well,
We'd make do with the shoe-sized pothole
Because it was also dependable,
Unless Dumbrowski's dad parked his green four door Rambler
To far from the curb again.
Then we'd be forced use the driver's side back door,
Of course, no one would dare touch it,
And you couldn't throw to third in that case
Unless you wanted some hell to pay
If the ball, even so much as harmlessly, bounced off that car.

The teams were as even as we could make them,
After all, where was the fun of blow-outs?
There'd be no arguing, hoopla, close calls, or tight situations.

We kept track of the innings, the score,
And chance was our umpire.
All disputes, not won by acclaim,
Or out blabbing by the dozens …
Were then settled by shooting odds and evens,
Or, flipping a fair coin for take-overs.
We had ways … and means … we had fun.
This was our street … as diamond!

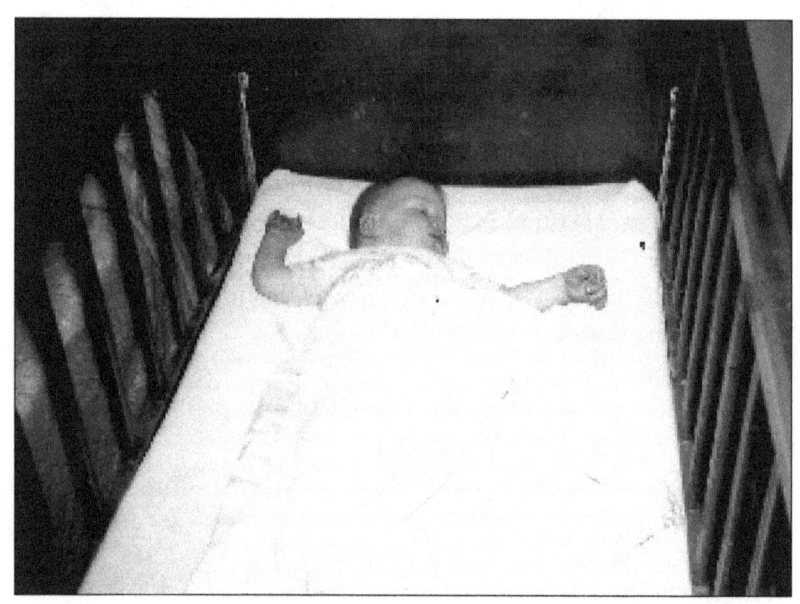

Here I am 9 months. This photo prompted a memory, probably the oldest one I have, that of being in a playpen and resting for a long time. I looked out an open window to a clear sky and appreciated every wan cool breeze, as it was very hot. Years later, Mom told me there had been a heat wave and I'd rested so much I had to relearn how to walk.

Memoirs Frozen In Memory

* "Warren R" was what we called him
But he was a Brunkey really
What I remember now is this
His coming up to me in his push-pedal car
His dusty face tear streaked
With a snotty nose
Hyper-ventilating
Between his sobs I understood
No one would play with him
So ... I did ... that time anyway

* After dinner, with all the lights out,
The reflections of candles
On the blue tile backsplash
Over the sink
These portending each birthday cake

* Picking out two big, cool, green sour dill pickles
That Izzy sold – two for a nickel
Kathy, my sister, paying him
To show me how good they were

* The soda truck
Broken down in the middle of the block
The man asking US to watch it for him
It was summer; it was hot
It was New York City
It was the three best six packs of Orange Crush
I ever had

* Watching my swollen leg reddening
The pus oozing out of a small, red, painful slit
My Mom swabbing as needed
Everyone mystified   Dad on the phone
Brothers and sisters at the doorway   silent

* After understanding Dad had let go
Yelling, "Look at me ... look at me!"
Passing by the house on my first two wheeler
To my first skid mark, Tom nodded
Saying, "You'll be a good driver."

* Bumper cars
Coney Island's boardwalk ... we,
In our excessive rambunctious joy,
Brought in the crowds
So the operator started letting us go free
Round after round

* Walking along behind Tom
He had decided on Rocky Road
Now, I liked the chocolate
Nibbled the marshmallows singly
But spit out all the walnuts ... secretly
While agreeing about how good it was

* The Christmas of Five Trees – a story I should write:
Everyone thought Mom wasn't going to buy one
So, in a handful of conspiracies, we all pitched in ...
And had five trees – we even put one in our bedroom!

* Calm summer afternoon; my Mom's scream
She'd found Jim's collection
Of snakes, lizards, mice and more
In our bedroom
All in the bottom of our dresser drawer
As she was putting clothes away

* Groggy with anesthesia ... oxygen tent ... cold
Raw throat   Mom's face ... brightening
So thirsty I "inhaled the water"
Achy in pain ... wondering what the heck is next?

* In light rain
Unable to see for tears
Unable to fathom loss
My brother's gravestone
Drops running out of his name

* My wife
In her wedding dress
In a breadth of sunshine
She paused for a moment … the sudden stillness
My breath taken away
A loss for words … lost in her smile
In the moment … the hush of time!

* New Year's Eve
We ascended the hill
Looked to the Pacific
Its deep purpling sea
Speckled with whitecaps
Above that a broad band
Of pure gold
Above that
A florid and fiery sunset raged
While chill air
Whispered about our feet in brown withered grass

* At Ocean Beach
For the millionth time
Her footprints, mine
Our silly messages
Drawings … assemblages
Left to the wind, the sand … and the tides
Holding hands … still warm
A rising wind deciding us –
We turned to see the sunset
In each other's eyes

* That first computer
Arranging its placement and that of the keyboard
Attaching the mouse
Booting it up – manual in hand
How many thousands of times – since
How many thousands of hours –
Altogether since?

* At my elementary school's fundraiser
The "Grand Potluck"
Mom says, "With all the different food set out
How come you are just eating my spaghetti and meatballs?"
I told her, "I know what I like and I go for the best."

* Ok, bike tag … the rules
"Well, it's just like regular tag
You know …
Except you're on a bike
And you had to tag him with your hand."
There was an element of danger
Nobody had helmets

* The rules for "Fireball 500, Follow that Car"
Yelling that was the signal to start
The target rider got a loud ten-count head start
Then everyone else chased them down
No rules
All against one – anything goes
You had to bring the wild rider down
No matter lawns, lots, gardens, or traffic
The best part?
If you tagged him first, you got to go next!

* The clear glass cross of holy water
From when we lived in New York City, it stood for years
Atop the wall heater in the hallway

* The hand sized, plastic, ivory colored,
Glow in the dark Jesus, I touched up with black ink
Accenting its outlines, the folds of the robe –
Was only given one eye

* After the many hospitalizations the final surgery
I began getting over hypodermics – at least a bit
Because of the pain which would wake me and take me over
And because the painkiller
Worked so beautifully
Would let me slip back into sleep
The opiate … was freedom … so warm … so good

* Riding the yellow barrel shaped marker buoys
Used to demarcate the beaches
It would bounce, buck and sway
In the small breaking waves … off Jamaica Bay
"Sea Biscuit" we called it
Riding the wild thing
Like a cowboy … like a clown
As an idiot child goofing … laughing
Until we fell off and got dunked
Over and over … the time of our lives
Mary, Kathy, Tom and I all taking turns

* Mom wrapped big towels around us, rubbed us dry,
And we would change underneath
While standing on the beach … into our clothes
That had been set out in the sun
Feeling traces of sand trickle down my leg
The warm sand beneath my feet

* A shell used
To hear the ocean
Until   far away
On a cloudy day   up in the garret
When it's memory   was found … again …

* Street Tag
With pieces of broken drywall – chalk
We'd outline an amazing maze
Paths, streets, zones, and short cuts
Chutes and ladders
Stopping places for hops or counts
Going backwards, on one foot or both
Shooting odds and evens   going to jail and more
The street – was the field for the game
Made … as we … went … along with it

From left to right: Danny, Johnny, who is holding my younger brother Jim, I believe, then Kathy, and Tom.

Way Back East

There was a time, long ago now, when I thought the world was safe. This despite those air raid sirens and being taught to duck and cover in elementary school. As far as I was concerned, the sirens meant getting under your desk, facing away from the windows, but most importantly, it was a break, albeit very brief, from the usual flow of classroom events. God knows what that did to my generation, psychologically speaking, but I didn't know what they really meant until I grew up.

I remember finding a fifty-cent piece; I mean to say this was really big money. With that in hand I ran off planning to go to a matinee, have a giant buttered popcorn, and had no idea what I'd do with all that I'd have left over.

Well, after the film let out, there I was walking along some large street, not far from home, when the sirens went off. I looked up in at sky but it was clear and beautifully blue, that's still my favorite color. I looked across the street at this brick building of maybe eight or ten stories because the sound seemed to be coming from it. I looked for a place to duck and cover but I was out in the open so I stood my ground, partly because no one else was running for cover.

When the blaring cut off, I felt all grown up and confident. I hadn't needed my two older brothers, my older sister, and all my friends on 207th street. I knew how to take care of myself, yeah! I had crossed big streets. I knew to look both ways, twice, and always let some one else start on across before you go and then, even then as I cross, to look around, you never know, as my Mom said. After all, I was a New Yorker, a Yankees fan, a good kid, and a Brady for god's sake. All of those things were something to be proud of but most importantly I hadn't been scared at all and felt big with my adventure!

Best of all, I had successfully completed my mission; I'd seen a movie on my own! On my way home, I remember spending some of my remaining treasure on the biggest chocolate bar in the world. I ate it but regretted not having enough money for a cool cap gun.

By the time I got home on that magical day it was a late afternoon. The street was full of kids playing just about every made up game you could imagine. The adults were sitting on their stoops in groups visiting, chatting, laughing and my Dad was on our stoop smoking his pipe. I hadn't been missed during my treasure-fueled adventure. I had gotten lucky, saw a movie, eaten my fill of chocolate, and had come back a hero – even if in my mind.

Yes, I was a hero even though no one knew it. I had energy and ran circles around the smaller kids. Then I insisted upon joining the stick ball game, then in progress. This time they said I could. Well I should have been MVP because I hit the ball twice, got on base and came home both times, caught a long fly ball for an out, and helped make a double play! I was in like Flynn. I knew it; just as I knew life would never be the same. I had made it to the big kids' game and there was no going back.

When I Was Growing Up

We lived in a three-story house.
On 207th Street, near Andrew Jackson High School
In New York City.

The top floor, the garret,
Was where we three older boys slept and
It was unfinished – but we liked it that way
There was nothing breakable up there
And plenty of room for pillow fights.
Also, as long as we didn't break the box springs,
We could bounce on our beds to beat the band
And neither Mom nor Dad would know.
We could sneak onto the roof, which was really cool,
Except for that one time when Tom began to slide off
And I barely got a hold on his arm
If John hadn't gotten there just in time, well.
That wasn't Tom's only close call growing up, believe me,
But we never told anyone that one, until now that is.
The floor below us had a bathroom and the other bedrooms
Mom and Dad's, the girls, and one for the youngest boys.

The ground floor had a side entrance, which led to the kitchen,
Which was big enough for the stove, the counter with its sink,
The refrigerator, and a nice kitchen table.
On that table was an old Philco radio set
And sometimes we listened to Gun Smoke as we ate.

There was the very big living room and
One other room on that floor, The Front Room,
Where we never went – ever.
It was always kept clean, quiet, and orderly.
If a guest came to the front door,
And one of us was allowed to let them in,
This was the first room they'd see.

It had an easy chair, a name I did not understand,
A very nice sofa, and a coffee table,
Another name I did not understand.
I mean to say, I smelled it – and it was nothing special.

Also, there were a few pictures on the wall;
That's all I can remember.

As I say, we rarely did more than peek into it.
It was, after all, The Front Room.
And God help anyone who messed it up, in any way.
You see, first you'd have to get away with it –
Meaning none of the other six kids could know that YOU did
Whatever it was
Because if they did you'd have to pay for silence or,
Failing that,
Face the trial with Mom and, after that,
The one with Dad.
And so, I ask you, rhetorically I mean,
What could possibly be worth all that?

There was also, in the back yard,
A real carriage house –
Yet another name I did not understand –
And that was where the bikes were kept,
And the sleds
And all manner of boxes and crates.
That, in sum was the house
And the rooms
That I remember.

Invisible Inheritance

Dad died in November – long after midnight

The morning after,
When I looked out our garret window,
Snow had fallen
And it was quiet outside as well.

Inside me was a dreamy calm –
While, in the house, a peculiar hush prevailed
It wasn't a problem,
In and of itself, for me
But I didn't know about anyone else –
And I didn't ask.

By the time we were all up,
It had become a silence thick enough to cut.

In the front room,
His big chair was never used thereafter.
His collection of records in the basement,
The many long shelves of glass 78's,
Something I'll never forget,
Were destined to disappear
But I didn't know it on that day.

I don't remember much about what happened
In the days after he died
However, I did avoid his funeral
Just by lagging behind
And going unnoticed
As everyone else piled into the cars.

I wish I could recall his last words to me.
There was nothing but change upon change afterwards

And then came the big move out to California
There I learned to disguise myself,
Blend in with silence, use passivity as camouflage,
And ignore feelings or wants,
Burying all such –
In order to hide in plain sight.

No one ever noticed.
This became a way
Of becoming
Who I became lo these many decades –

After the move,
I took to looking up at stars
Not to wish on them
But to wonder and, more than once,
Cry both blind and hard,
Because I understood I'd never get up close to one of them
Or any heavenly body.

As an adult,
Living on the edge of the continent,
At home in my secret, silent, solitude,
I kept to my own world
As if by holding on to just me
I could avoid the consequences of the past
While, by the same token,
I never lost contact with it,
What it became for me
Or what I became because of it –

Over the years,
I took, in hand, in heart,
And into my soul …
My invisible inheritance.

My Father is third from the left. The man giving him a hug is his uncle, Charlie Shannon. Mom is to the right of him, in the back row, and hard to see.

Father's Day Card

My father passed on 45 years now.
And I am glad to think of him
I don't hold anything against him,
I was just turning seven
When he had a heart attack

He once worked in a bar
In New York City
There's a black and white picture
And I can tell it's him
The family face is clear enough
A cousin found it and sent it out to me

In another, he's wearing a suit
A good suit
With a backdrop depicting a park
He's smiling
It must have been a Sunday
The way his hair was combed neat as a pin
And his shoes shone

In another he's wearing an army uniform
Straddling a Harley
And in another he's with his unit
And they're all mugging it up
Anonymous blurry faces
Recognizable only to their relatives
He was in Alaska during World War Two
Saw action in the Aleutian Islands
Years later, in our garage,
My oldest brother found it
The chopper, a Thompson sub-machine gun,
With its round cartridge full of 45 caliber rounds
Boy, did he get in trouble.

The day before the night he passed on
He gave the seven of us kids a big handful of change
We went to see "Darby O' Gill and the Little People"
And I got to tell you I was scared of that banshee
I warned Mom and Dad
Who went see it themselves after dinner

That night   silence woke me up

My brothers' beds were empty
A flashing orange light
Repeatedly swept across the window
And there was talking down stairs, quiet talking
It was long, long after bedtime –
Which for us, back then, was 8:30pm

We stayed at home the next day
I remember playing inside
Because all the other children
Were at school.

Some years later, my mother, in teary recollection,
Told me about that morning
She said she seen a ghostly image of herself
Laughing, pointing at her
Mocking her for trusting
That life could go on and be good
And blaming her
For being left with the seven of us.

Soon we moved from New York City and to Fremont,
In a dream I saw our housing tract
The squared sections of redwood fencing
And the sort of puzzle piece arrangement
Which made up the streets and blocks.

Dad never had to deal with Tom's death in Vietnam
To question my questioning of that war
Worry about Kathy's career as an actress
Go ballistic regarding Mary's marriage
Charlie's wild oats or Jim's for that matter.
He'd never get the chance
To reminisce with John
About war and how SNAFU it is
He would never see the times-a-changing
As Dylan sang of them,
The lie of Vietnam,
The back-to-back Iraq attacks,
No, he'd never get to sit around and complain
About how they've botched it
How his buddy's sons or grandsons
Have lost patience   or complain
About the direction this country has been goaded into
I am glad he passed, when he did
He didn't have to see
The egregious losses from his generation
Being used as fodder
In speeches by an escape artist
To promote a failure touted as success
He wouldn't have to sit and yell at the TV
Or mumble in his sleep wishing he were dead
Rather then see the sacrifices
He and his generation made
Flushed down the memory hole
By persons who've never heard
The distinct whine of a 45 caliber bullet zipping by
Or the spattering thud it makes when it's stopped by flesh.

No, he lived long enough
Just through the 50's and most of Ike
He had a good life really
Enjoying the time before reality began to split

And come undone
First by the young and the old and then
By war and peace
By white and non-white
By the first, second, and third worlds
The pill and condom
Music and the sound of silence
Lyrics and politics
By born again and the simply born
By science and pulpits
Perception and reality
Sound bites and spin meisters
Capitalism and simple greed
Lies masquerading as truths
Truths held as lies
Or even time itself
Where memories become one's redoubt
A soft refuge where dreams become their illusions
My father died young
That's what the doctors say
But I think
He went with his time
And only suffered briefly
Paying the price that his diet demanded
Not knowing, until the shuddering
That his marker had been called
And not knowing how or why
He died as Mom called his name
As she shook him and understood
He'd never reply to that last comment of hers
That the warm tears which she let
And which broke on his face   were unfelt
He could not see how she dried them
Before going to the phone
Before getting all us kids up
To let us know that our childhood was over.

Charlie Shannon, his niece Catherine Brady, nephew Charlie Brady, son Rev. Phil Shannon, niece Katie O'Reilly. 1940s NYC

I was given my first and middle names courtesy of two priests in the family, the Reverends Philip and Daniel Shannon. Because their church records, I was able to find the connection to my grandmother, on the Shannon side of the family, who was born in Ireland.

****

Chapter Two

60/6 – 72/9   Fremont, Washington High, Ohlone J.C.

After Dad died, my Mom moved us from New York City to Fremont California. She had been born in or near Sacramento to immigrant parents. Her mother died and her father remarried. She told me that her stepmother was cruel. As a young woman, prompted in part by dysfunctional family conditions, she left home and lived in Oakland off High Street with a couple we children knew as Uncle Babe and Aunt Florence. It was Uncle Babe, Mr. Bruschini, who helped her resettle in Fremont. I remember her saying she liked the hills of Fremont and the way they changed color with the season as they reminded her of some portion of her childhood.

As for me, life was very different in Fremont California. I do remember entering the new house only to be very surprised that it was fully furnished, there were clothes, a TV, washer and drier, bedding, towels, food, and many more surprises. The word had gone out and the community responded magnificently. I, however, fell into being a recluse staying inside the house for days on end until my sister Kathy introduced me to a neighbor boy, Bobby. He and I became friendly toward one another. That said, I became solitary in my predilections, learned how to avoid conflict, connections, and keep to myself as a way of coping with the disappearance of my New York world.

This is us on an Easter a few yeas after we arrived. In the background, is John's 38 Buick Special, which dates the photograph. In the back row, from left to right, are Danny, Tommy, Kathy, John, and Mom, in the front row, are Jimmy, Mary, holding one of our many pets, and Charlie holding our famed cat, Tiger. We are at our home in Cabrillo Park, Fremont.

Summer Night

He was just seven years old
But talkative ... inquisitive too
And he had a way with words
Believe me

Tonight he was excited
And, for once, intently quiet

Long after hours, dinner and sunset
He was in the school's playground
Waiting with his dad and I
To look through a real telescope
Provided by the local astronomer's club

We'd decided to look at Andromeda

I stood by him looking forward to my turn as well
While his dad left to go get something from the car
When his turn came up,
I got down on my knee
To help him look through the eyepiece,
Watched his eye,
Saw, on its fluid surface, a point of illumination
This was Andromeda!

He saw – and I saw his wondering gaze
Study ...

I told him,
"That light is two million years old, and tonight,
Tonight it is here
Magnified by a simple set of lenses
Before it lands upon your eye,
Its lenses, focus it upon your retina

Where it's translated into electronic code …"

"Wow" he whispered.

"Then," I continued, "nerves, take that code
Back into your brain
To be reassembled to be seen for what it is …
In your mind
And that's what you really see!"

His wide-eyed sight was transfixed
In wonderment
Upon the ancient artifact, the data transformation,
Transition and other considerations or effects.
His mouth motioned a hushed "wow."

That night we saw
Something from a place so very far way,
And vastly ancient,
Brought right into our own here and now.
"It's like a time machine – of sorts," he said.
"Yes, it is and that light will make a memory
You can carry with you."

He smiled.

We were touched
We took … in … something

We both
Saw the light
On that summer's night
And that's something I'll never forget

Unusually Tall

I was unusually tall for my age
And stood out, as it were,
Becoming target of would be bullies,
Or proto-gangs, wanting me to have "a piece of the action."
I never understood the attraction …
And learned to disappear into their assumptions,
Occlude their perceptions,
Creating an invisibility cloak no one saw – or saw through.

This provided me a refuge, a redoubt,
And I was safe in solitude for decades.
If I did ever accept invitations, out of habit,
I would survive any party house's game of thrones,
Play the jokester,
Flirt with terms of endearment,
Take a chance on a dance,
Give or take the party-eye glance,
But I was an escape artiste for all that
And could put on the best poker face
When called upon to deliver
Quietly happy I was never seen for what I was.

No matter how distant I had to become,
I could go that distance –
Anything to be safe.
So there was a period I called the golden age
When, for years on end, I had all the space I needed
Being successfully camouflaged
From the chaos of socializing.
Over those decades I went farther and farther
Becoming so usually unusual
That I felt safe, enjoyed being becalmed and at ease.
I remember one time when, outside of work,
I averaged less that five words a day.

And was very happy with that.
To paraphrase Aristotle
"Give me a place to stand …
And I can avoid … the universe"

Yet, eventually,
When whatever had set me on that path
Could no longer be seen,
Or remembered,
There came a time
When my inherent, heartfelt need,
To be fully alive and free of those inchoate fears,
Long harbored, and secreted
And a longing to express feelings,
Became much more important
Than simple protection or safe-keeping.
Over time,
With trepidation, at first, and then with some certainty,
I found the long and winding way out –
I was an escape artiste after all.

Over the course of some years,
I learned to put my heart at risk –
And am deeply grateful
For the love that came my way
And how she led me to become someone else altogether
Therefore, I harbor no regrets
Concerning my escape from my redoubt … my refuge,
And that's the truth.

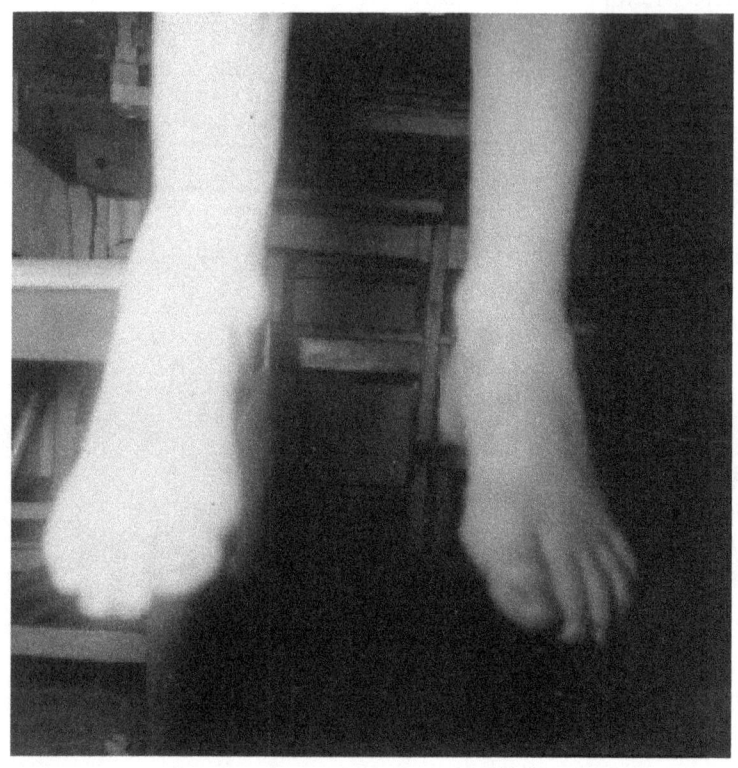

Mom took this picture of my right ankle as it started to show the deforming impacts of the disparate growth rates of my two lower leg bones – although this photo does not show that well. This disability changed my life in many profound ways, a process that continues to this day.

Legendary

When I missed him
It was long, long after he'd made a song out of my name,
Long after he'd removed those training wheels,
When I turned to look and see if he'd let me go on my own
Decades after I must have held his hand for the last time
Or that time when he asked if I wanted to help with the lawn
Or hearing him say, "You can do it!"

Not meaning to demean Mom or others who helped me
Without my knowing it, sometimes
Without my asking, almost always
And who disregarded my thanks, kindly enough ...
To mentors Tommy and Johnny
And a few odd ball others:
Mr. Ernst, my 4th grade French teacher,
Mr. Kitajima, middle school science teacher,
Mr. Otto Graf, high school science teacher,
And Mr. Steinke, professor of philosophy at Ohlone

After some decades of oblique silence
There came a time when I came prayed each night
For everyone in my family ... I made it a practice
But it was months before I realized I'd forgotten him
On that night, when I added prayers for him,
I heard his voice saying, "Well, it's about time!"
And that's the last I ever heard from him

When, more recently, I saw a movie,
Its name is not important,
But its theme was how, again and again, variously
People pass love along
Not only through an embrace ... nor kiss
Or even saying that word
But by acting on the impulse to give
Believe, trust, share, care or just be there

Unwavering and determined to be of use
Again and again, the players were willing
To sacrifice something considered real
For that which is beyond the reach of every sense you have

Save one

And so in a darkened cinema
I had cause to thank him ... once more

I had my brimming illumination ... and understood
How my heart teaches every day,
Bears its delicate intimacy,
And reminds ... reminds
As if I could ever forget,
That I am a son
Who has a father
Whose regard for me remains as vital
As any breath I take
And whose love
Is as warm
As any tear I care to shed

Your Favorite Pet?

Well, I thought of Tiger
The gold and white-striped tabby of my childhood
I don't remember how he found our home
One of us could've had him, "follow me home!"
He could've been chosen from a set of mewling mites
Happily playing in the childishly plush confines
Of a large cardboard box
Wedged into a little red wagon of a Saturday morning

He was legendary though
Surviving that car accident,
The vet, taking pity on him ... on us,
Wired Tiger's jaw back together
Set his back leg, carefully casting it and more
And money, always and issue at our house,
Didn't seem to be an object when it came to saving his life
And that says something too

Once on a summery kind of Sunday evening
He brought the neighbor's rooster to dinner
Which our neighbors bought to keep Tiger off their hens,
A failed plan,
And there was the attempted theft of a full roast
Off the dining room table,
The downing of a hawk, and running off dogs

Then too, there were those evenings,
When, as the family quietly TeeVeed,
I'd be in the back room
Steeping in my kind of solitude
Reading, writing, or playing chess
When Tiger would seek me out

He once walked through a game of chess
Not touching a single piece and purring as he did so

Just ... to go nose to nose

He was a healer too, I remember
He'd clamber up to the top of the sofa
Stalk along behind our heads before settling down
Behind someone's head and

Drooping himself
Across their shoulders   to purr ... soothing
Warm and
Sweet ...

Tiger

The cat of cats ...

Who is legend!

This is a picture from 8th grade, at Thornton Junior High in Fremont. I was there for a dress up dance event – a long story there. I didn't want to go, but Mom went through all the motions in getting me that coat, a clip on bow tie, and she reminded me about going. That night, when she came home from work, and saw I was still there – she rushed me into the suit and got me there in plenty of time. I, painfully shy, was extremely uncomfortable almost the entire time but I told her I had had fun when I had not. She asked me if I had danced and I said I had. She was glad; I was relieved as the illusion of a happy experience to continued for all concerned.

Gold

Gold catches my eye;
During sunset, it is the most rare of elements.

When I was young,
But not very young,
I had a large magnifying glass
And I held it up
Between my face and the bathroom mirror,
Curious to see what would happen.

Mom had always told me my eyes were hazel.
I enjoyed the sound of that word
As well as my understanding
Of what she told me it meant.
But, that day,
I was surprised as could be
When, in them, I saw sky blue, my favorite color,
A bright new-grass kind of yellow-green,
As well as deep emerald points.
There were browns, of course, greys,
And wilder colors, violet, magenta
And, flecks of pure gold!
Why, the whole rainbow was in them, and more!
I was flabbergasted
And so shocked
That, for some reason,
I never told anyone
Ever
Not until now,
That is.

One lesson from this may be
That you never know what form inspiration may take,
Nor, for that matter, where it will take you,

What connects to what,
Or what was to what will be,
Or what becomes of becoming what becomes of becoming.
Another lesson, maybe, is
That one is never far away from one's past.
What with a single word, gold, in this case
Setting me off to run along a trail
That took me smack back to something
I had long forgotten.

Or, another lesson, but certainly not the last,
By a long shot, I'd wager,
Is that time has nothing to do with memory
As this instantly connected reflection demonstrates.
Time may be what we imagine connects
What we were, are, or may yet be;
It might just be what we think it is,
Or something else altogether.

One other thing, and this is the final item,
Cutting to the chase, as it were.
Time has nothing to do with the lesson
That lessons go on and on and on
Despite the fact that they always bring us
Back to the present moment
At almost the exact same time as when we left …
Such as what happened with this poem … here
As well as with you, reading this,
Considering the meaning
That gold has
For you!

What I Wear ... Not

What I wear   my knot
Nikes not my knot
My gender, not my knot – but not
What's a boy or girl   but a knot of nots?
Ethnicity my knot and not, yours ... and not
Arab, a knot   mine and others'
My religion, not my knot but everyone else's
Muslim, not my knot
Nationality, not my knot
American, knot
Eat, what a knot
School, my knot and not my knot
Classmates not my knot
Test scores, my knot and, then again, not
Beautiful eyes – a knot
Smooth skin – my knot
Music – my knot
Books, not my knot
Laughter, a knot and then again not a knot
Can you see now what is or is not a knot?
Touch – can you or can't you –
A knot and not a knot or visa versa
Are we all about knots, learn knots, talk not of knots,
Hear or hear not knots
Me, about knots and not
Measure, you can not –
Anything I am not – even knots
Me, seeing you, thinking you know what knot I am or not
Seen not – I am
I know – a kind of knot of nots
Not known for knots or not, you too
Known not for knots or not
Love – not love
Love knots

Why (not) love?
Love – why (not)
I don't know –
You pick that one
But, I digress myself
Into distractions   in sum
Love, from what I have seen –
Is lots of knots
But really not at all, a knot – even when tied
Into knots knotted in knots of knots

Understood or not
Understanding or not
Knots of knots and the nots of knots in the way
In any way   yours, mine and ours
Of what I understand
Not clear: knots of knot knotted – not
I am not what your knots knot me into
To be or a knot not to be   knots
That is my question   not

What Comes Of The Long Lost

Apropos of nothing, sadness wells – and heavily so
"Oh, Mom," I mutter to myself.

In one old photo, she stands arms spread wide,
A gesture that included all us kids, around and behind her
She wore the smile we all still use
And, in full sunlight,
One can clearly see the family nose, brow, and forehead
Imprinted on each of us Bradys.

On the other hand
This lamp, in my office now, was a gift
Originally from the charities,
Which provided her,
The widow with seven,
With the many cast off furnishings,
Which welcomed us to our Fremont home –
When she'd expected absolutely nothing
Knowing that the moving van hadn't even left New York.

Back then, dressing for Sundays
Was the only option.
We all did our best,
From shoes to hair.
And checked each other to be exact.
Her smile being the reward.

There was a time, years later,
When with laundry covering half the big dining room table
With her books, binders of class notes taking up the rest,
She worked it full on –
Through regrets,
Struggles with time and fate,
Pushing herself through two jobs,

Raising the seven of us, and full-time schooling.
How many hours, days, weeks
Months, and years even
Could be read in any one of her questioning looks?

Still now … this winter
Well after she has been gone …
I take note of her
As I, once more,
Reminisce
On all those things
That might have been
When,
In the bathroom mirror
That smile
With so many secrets
Is seen yet again
On me.

Mr. R. Bruschini

in his chair he
would just say
pretty kitty – pretty kitty
wave a finger up
and the cat would,
after years, know
when to be there
just before he'd ask
she'd be listening
staring out
for the sounds he'd make
just before he'd think she'd be listening
and she'd know
before he'd be ready
she'd know

he would sit
the afternoon
a long dog barks away
moving his hand over
her shoulders stroking her flanks
he rolls her cheeks, rubs her chin
and she arches her head and back on his lap,

all those times
he touches
her eyes closed

– her ears flutter

  – this time

   – this time

     – he wouldn't make an appointment

– wouldn't

   – go to the garage –

     – warm up the car – or

have to explain to someone who asked after her
how the time had left with her

he sits in the chair
in the sun
in the afternoon
long dog barks away
with window light
half on his face

My Uncle

I remember, I remember him
he was just, here
in the garden
the way touched plants
and watched the children
turn and spin the day, as if
with their faces to the sun
they themselves were in bloom
as his carnations are now

and his cat
I remember
would always jump right up on his lap expecting
finding sleep
for hours in the afternoon Sunday sky falls to autumn

I remember the family dinner
in the Italian kitchen he
would always make a salad
sprinkled with everything colors
all on the lettuce, he'd bring it in the wooden bowl
a debut of immigrant pride
with a smile his grandfather wore

Dream Doctor

They told me that I knew the way.
They came in the hospital;
I walked with them out of the room.
Walking was no problem;
To explain my walking through the wall was;
A matter of listening so intently
That you follow the sound back inside
To its origin;
Bearing this way was to be outside.

I said,

"But I thought it would take longer;
I thought that I'd have to get (((their)))
On my own."

But they said,

"No, all you have to do is lie down,
Slip over the edge, and go flat out!"

the cat hops on the table
walks carefully   through the chess game
sniffs at my nose

        in the hot shade
            between corn stalks
                the pile of sleeping kittens

ants come to it   go
over, around and all about
the pebble   in their hole

        Elderberry Park   water strider
    A kick
Ripples   the moon

This is Tom at his graduation from Basic Training at Fort Ord, California in 1967.

This is the last picture of Tom. It was taken at my Uncle Babe's home in Oakland just before he shipped out. I am partly seen on the right leaning against Mom's car when Babe took the photo.

her late visit,
glance, and hesitation   telling
my heart   the news   his death

That dollar thirty seven
That change in his pocket
That last day ... Vietnam

It's summer again
the president is live
on TV
answering news
man's questions
and I
watch my brother
the one who is growing
lettuce, swiss chard, onions, tomatoes, corn, beans
and brussel sprouts
in our backyard
it is quiet
dust
between the corn stalks
and the chard will taste like it sounds
in the earth in the summer
in my brother's
growing hands

*Note, my younger brother Charles is
assumed in this piece.*

Valedictory

June favors your faces now.
Its soft wind is hardly felt.
Your eyes not only reflect
But glitter with youth therein
On this promised day of prospect.
You are with friends, family
Co-workers and teachers all.
Take a deep breath inside.
And as I read this passage
Take your pulse, measured without pride.

Why? For I begin with death
Which should be far away and
Unconsidered at such a time.
Yet this is where I begin
With my true intent sublime.
This dire soulful matter
Ever lays so close to hand.
It forms us, as does life's run;
In that how we speak of it
Tells on us each and every one.

While you feel that beat within,
Your measure so sure and steady,
Consider what you might say,
If your dearest lay before you failing
Or yourself had but one last day.
In memory time is never; it is not
So let us seize moments this day
To take and hold our friends dear
Knowing chance or circumstance
Will take some from us within the year.

You may wish to hear no more.
But failing to consider your end,
Is to ignore what I mean:
Which is to say, how you will measure
Careers through which you'll careen.
For each of you will answer
As to how you've lived your life,
If you've stood the test of time
To be counted a success
As you viewed such here, in your prime.

To deny or ignore death?
Is to impact your reason.
Fear it and you'll live in dread
Squandering what you'll call life until
Until only your legacy is coveted.
You need only think ahead
To pass life's common dangers by.
The addict's escape or zealot's stance
For each of these remedies are given;
But there is no cure for chance.

No insurance can answer
For injuring accident
Even if the error or fault is clear.
Being a victim of a random act
Would you hold your suffering life dear?
Synchronicity and kismet,
Vagaries of time and place,
Will your seed be one that's sown
Will you be meet with passion's swell
Or travel the long and winding road alone?

Yearbooks fade in a closet.
Their pictures no longer tell
Anything that might have been said
When they knew you so long ago
When their skin blushed red.
Years pass and your numbers fall.
As one by one you lay forgotten
Beneath a stone upended in the ground,
Perhaps to be named at a reunion
Between brief pauses in sound.

While proud youth can claim the answers
Or boast of their newfound views
I ask which would be more strange
To have all your findings hold, or
That, over time, your mind will change?
Enough for now, be about yourself today.
And as you take these first steps,
Think through them to the future unseen,
Consider how you might, by knowing thyself,
Certain of life's treasures, glean.

Find the solace of your heart
And take its love whithersoever you go.
This abides through every good or ill
And, as intimate as your pulse,
It is to be your own life's codicil.
Know your death is an ending
Only if your life has missed its mark.
If you'd outlast your funerary knell
To leave life rippling in your wake
Pass along the precious gifts eternal.

Know that as you give so you create.
But one must do more than simply suffice
For all that pales when compared to the best:
Will you leave a legacy of truth
Will your name stand that acid test?
Say what you will of that now,
But be truthful then, if only to yourself,
When perhaps you've lost your way
That you will hear your heart's voice
As it would speak to you from this day.

Life takes you on many roads
And chance deals out your hand;
The easy treasures are too soon spent.
Hold the dreams of your secret harbor dear
Keep your soul sweet and penitent.
Then some day in the distance
We'll stop, as we chance to meet
Will you then be at the fore
And, true to yourselves today,
Enriched humanities store?

At a glance we'll know what's true.
Will you be known for giving?
And always been worthy of trust?
Did you live up to today's promise?
Or will you just be leaving more dust?

Of course, I was nowhere near to being the valedictorian, but this was written about that idea, some decades later as an amendment or a way of saying what I would say now – were I asked.

Looking

Looking into a mirror
Looking into my eyes
Considering this reflection –
Will hardly make me wise

Looking into what I see
Looking through the disguise
Considering my apprehension –
Will affect what I realize

Looking into memory
Looking at what I recall
Considering renovation –
And what must go before a fall

Looking over my tales
And their cinched up lies
Considering my intent –
Will, and loosing those ties

Looking and sifting clues
Looking to sum or surmise
Considering full restitution
Will I be done before my demise?

To ask myself if this is difficult
no
this is
easy
sitting with time and tea at the window
how the glass meets the wind
now that time of report card signing seems immediate
brows fevered cooling
measles now
washing clothes now
meals
their cooking
and planning
always planning so
difficult
yet I was not lost somehow
I am still
worried
sad or   somehow
are they reading between the lines of my face?
I receive pretty cards and notes

Miles and holidays
it's called
a generation gap

Do they know me now?
I understand them
they understand
I am still

feel and

One
by one ...
birds cross blue skies ...

I watch from my window

frost

one by one
the leaving
colors fall to the brown earth smooth as skin
I notice the gaps
between my fingers
the shape of the spaces
notice a ring
a man
and memories

In the autumn

it is difficult
I accept
three children grown
and married

                    June   high noon
        between table planks   in cobweb
                 One glistening dewdrop

  The wind   the rain –
  this wet sidewalk   snail you
   out on a night like this

It was the saddest day of my life when we went to see Tom's grave. It was deeply traumatic. I had all the more reason to detach and seek out my dear redoubt. It was some 25 years before I could go to his grave and not cry. Then, for a time, when I visited the site, I'd talk as if we were together, hanging out, and shooting the breeze!

This grainy image was what I found online from his high school record. He was in the debate club, studied German as a foreign language, read a great deal, and sent me Bob Dylan records when he was training at Fort Benning, Georgia. He went to officer's candidate school and would likely have succeeded had it not been for an injury or an illness, which took him out of the program long enough to prevent further effort. As it was, he became a sergeant, just as Dad had.

Spoiler Alert: the following poems were written in high school between the years 1966 and 1970. I am including these because they are historical and have themes that have reoccurred throughout out much of my writing from then until now.

Say what you feel
Feel what you say
Those who do this
Live in a happier way

We, You, and I

The one between
Through which we see us

A new light
A new sense
More than I or you – us

Real

From switch to switch
Channel to channel
Channel to chair
And chair to chair
We travel and yearn for what is real

We know with recordings, tape, and print
Think with bubbles and punch holes
And we continue on along
As I do my best
Leaving reality alone
A problematical pest

How long will you last
And after you've gone
How many will know you've passed?
Your loves, hopes, needs
Your fears and deeds
How many will care?
How many?
What will you leave as a milestone
The deeds you've done?
The seeds you've sown?
I'll tell you, my friend, I'll tell you
An obscure weed ridden patch
Marked by a weathered, broken stone.

Did you ever
While staring into the depths of blue
Lose your body
Sense that your arms, legs, and head
Are askew?

Strewn   strange and distant
They look wholly odd and new

Something

Where are all the oaks on Oak Street?
Where are the beech in Beechwood Park?
The thing I ask is just this
Why are the streets
With the flowery names so stark?

This poem has the distinguished honor of having been published in "Senator Bilbo's Fodel" the 1970 senior class literary and art magazine – ah, memories!

Beer can in the gutter reflecting at me
There for all the world to see
Beer can, what a sight
Beer can, what a sight
Beer can lying there where the grass should be
Killing all the greenery
Lift them up and nothing but barren earth do you see
Beer can, it's just not right
Beer can, it's just not right
Empty beer can of use it's devoid
It does not know the beauty it has destroyed
Beer can, what a sight
Beer can, reflects our plight

****
Chapter Three

72/9 – 75/8   San Francisco State

This was only a four-year stretch but it was the first time I was truly on my own. With the help of a good and life-long friend, Jim G., I learned how to find a place to live, get a job, and manage my simple set of affairs. For a while I lived on Jules Avenue and this was where I first self-identified as a poet, co-created Birthstone Magazine, began going to open mics, and sent pieces out for publication.

I landed my first full-time office job at the National Automobile Club and held that job for several years. I was not well known amidst the circles I traveled in, that is to say, for the most part and for most all this time.

The Dialogue:

You know
One day
I was sitting alone in my easy chair
The window was open
And the spring breeze was particularly sweet
The sun was streaming in
Keeping me warm
And I could lean back and rest
So I closed my eyes and did just that
There were some birds calling – the sound of leaves in trees
And dappled sunny colors played on my eyelids

Then,
Perhaps right as it was all perfectly peaceful,
And I was settled, comfy cozy
A few dream shapes flickered and memories whispered
The cat
Ever so lightly hopped up to my lap
Now, I didn't react … I was relaxing … easy …
And he seemed to understand
For he paused, lay down, and curled into sleep

I knew what he was thinking
"Ah, this is the life
Here's a nice big lap
Of a human dozer
It's a quiet day
I like that nice bit of breeze
We have some sunshine going on in here
And he's not going to be moving any time soon
Yup, I got some good naps in today
Chased some stuff
Played with that damned ball of his – but now
Now there is this

It just doesn't get any better than this."
I could tell all that
By the way he'd gotten up
And curled into a snuggle
Without looking
I knew his eyes were smilingly closed

So I whispered,
"Yup, I agree; it just doesn't get any better than this."
And the cat rubbed his head ever so slightly
Nuzzling my thigh …

I had a thought about something from work
And the cat stretched one paw – its claw caught – just a bit

I dreamt of the heavens
The sprawling magnificence of the jeweled firmament
He began a soft purr
And when I thought of a friend
He gave one of the softest meows I've ever heard
And so in conversation we remained
And so we traveled very far that day
This cat and I

And when I began to think about dinner
I felt his tail switch … I was sure of that
And when I yawned
He stretched   and then we both looked at each other
For a long and strange moment

Oh, we'd had our wonders before   our dialogues
More than once, but now, now
We both knew just one thing
It was certainly time for dinner!

On Campus

two or three years ago
I thought I'd send you
one of those records
a 45 from the 50's
with some man singing a woman so she wouldn't leave

put it in a big envelope
mark it fragile
stick a crowd of stamps on it
it would get to you
I hoped

I'd think about it now and then
it was months later

I saw you in a band's crowd
on campus
almost dancing at the edge crowd

a shock
when you looked at me
I hadn't forgotten
but I didn't remember
you
as someone
I knew

What I Never Told Mom:

When the gas
Was strengthening

And I,
Drunken, sprawled on my king sized bed,
Began to slip –
Away

I saw your drawn look go heavenward
And
Your eyes gleam –
Tears streaming …
It was the "oh" of your lip's   shaping a moan –
Which brought me to …

Had me "get up and …"
As you put it, "get on with it!"

So, I opened up windows
To air the place out
Took a deep indrawn breath from the cold draft
On that winter day
Long, long ago

This
Is what I never told you
And I'm sorry

on the Fillmore bus
this man's face
a study of fine lines
rough creases
rustling hands
in a twisted bag of pecans
his talk   a rambling monologue
wanders over and around to the housewife
whose green robe is too small and smudged
her feet bulge over her blue house slippers
he offers
holds the bag out
for her consideration
she
is well versed
a practiced listener
she knows enough to say
no

I'm on a special diet

with a smile   he returns
his attention
to the pecans at the very bottom
of the small bag

Black Hair Beaten

a face they called at
when she was young
her eyes were
always beyond the buildings and crowds

somewhere in her stride
there was a child
in 51
when she was young, 26
she had been a beat or whatever
they
were called, back then
for 10 years in New York
she rode buses

here, on a bus now
she begins to rummage her macramé carry all
spotted with different yarns and strings
that hold
the original Victorian house design, its ropes
and blue stones
still seen
for what it was.

The Last Time Ever I Saw Your Face

The blurry world
Ran with sparkling tear smeared colors
Not a one held back
No matter that I tried
But you turned away
Even as I did
Afraid we'd see each other's ...
Giving you a moment I then turned back
I watched as you diminished
Walking to the bus stop a very long block away
Before you were lost to sight
Then, I thought I saw your hat and coat
Thought, for a moment, you looked back
But neither of us gave a parting gesture
That was the last

Without anything better to do
I waited as the bus moved past me
I looked but did not see you; it was crowded
Not caring to move, I stood
Ignoring thoughts – dismissing heartbeats for some time

Reflecting on that last minute
When we stood, before you turned away,
Even then ... I could not tell you ... or ask
Or say what I wanted

So it was that our great silence was kept
Even as it had been all those years

We were, as it turned out, champions
At last long good byes what with crying we did not share
And keeping everything we ever wanted to give
Completely to ourselves

Even at the so-called bitter end
Even then, when one word
Could have made a difference
We could not
For the life of us
Say that one word
Even as our beating hearts
Trembled
Our faces blushed
And our eyes spoke eloquently ... longingly
But were mute for all that ...
Our lips   grimly set
Did not part
Were the same lips
Which never did move to meet
And which still
Still have nothing to say

a knife on the table having   sliced a tomato wet

sun by the window seeds on   a knife on the table

a sliced tomato

two voices in another room   vague

in the sunlight over the table

a sliced tomato   a knife   its blade   worn sharpening years

has no shadow

and the bowl   the plate

and time now   the sun   the knife

with dark stains and marks on the handle

outside the window a tree

at the stove above   the utensils move

metal pot and ladle   chimes

on the table the bread   unsliced waits

with the plate and bowl

and a knife on the table having

sliced a tomato

wet sun

blame the water drops leaking
blame the landlord
blame the economy or politicians
blame the Dodo
and its extinct feathers

wake up in the morning
brush your hair in fashion
with electrically heated air
power in your hands
call your friends
the gossip news
and where to place the blame
decide who to have over
for ice cream and soda
and go to a movie
or take in a dinner

spend time at the park
put the mustard on the hot dog
that has traveled more than you have
to get there
and then sit down with the trees

going over it all   you are tired
at home
read the magazine
all about the famous peek at them
see them with hats in fashion
at the airport as they are about to leave
dream of their private luxury airline cruising
above mountains
and shovel your souls weight
into their accounts

Being Okay

the bus ride a jumble of getting off work conversation
and she sits down next to me
we talk
she says she's nine months pregnant
due next week   smiles

I glance down
I want to touch her glowing curve
feel what's inside
to know this
but I say other things
just other things

If she'd shudder
what then
the rippling muscle
I'd have to use my hands to help her
afraid to be unable
I hold on to her
give a position of support from behind
her up on her knees
to let it fall out
I wipe her forehead of strain
I
talk   trembles down arms hands – warm
I hold it in mother's blood

at the stop
where she gets off
I mumble a good-bye
she smiles again
carefully managing the steps
she'll be okay ... so

so

how is it that later
I wait for sleep
reviewing every
moment
of that dream
asking what would I have done

what could I do?

outside my window
plants and trees silhouette
in the gathering dusk

cool air

wafts in

slowly   one deep breath

after another
slowly
one
deep
breath

everything echoes
in the men's room
and
I'm quite sure someone will overhear this

most will just go
thinking what they want
but
some guy
some guy will quietly out-loud wonder
"Just what are you doing in there
to make those tiny noises?"
sure enough
when I come out, sure enough
there he is
up against a wall, with his arms across his chest,
his looks heat my face

I know he thinks:
"Aha! He was the one who was in there doing it."
maybe he thinks I wrote on the walls or on the toilet
or that I was
I turn away
he has the wrong idea about me,
this
is what I was doing

A Hallmrak Card:

night so blue
starts so bright
snow so pure
snow so white
what a sight
in the night
falling down
as soft as light
the snow is pretty
the snow is fine
the snow: its' yours
the snow: its' mine.

His Melody

Oh, Diva … in descent
Whose delicious form
Comprised of naught but clouds
And unadorned appeared
Without a thought of garment
Whose countenance, torso …
Whose flower
Would have all feminine vanity cease
Whose gentle zephyr, spring's breath
Insinuates through the rank verge
Hints over the balustrade … or
Is found in the season's scent
Condensed thickly
Into the myriad of dew points
Depending from twigs
Speckling each leaf
Bowing every blade of grass
About this abode
If I recall, correctly,
The sight my vision beheld
Was from a lonely mountain's peak
Long, long ago and, at this stage of life,
If I do not find her here
In Jupiter's bejeweled palace of jasper
Then I would leave this elevated platform
To meander again
Beneath a wild and pale moon
Along that path
Beside the silvered waters
Of a darkling glen
And hope for a reprise of that encounter
Only starlit … Oh, Diva
How can I love another?

Eve

no rose
so soft so
succulent
as this red blush
that embarrasses you
no
dew as sweet
or welcome
as the gleam
of your laughter's eye
no wind
as soft
or cool as the breath
that leaves your lips
parted in sleep
your calm
dreaming hair
is a wonder
scarcely said
by one such as I
finding myself to be
too   too quiet
in your presence

This picture of Niels, from around this period. He was in Davis and I used to visit him up there. From high school onward we influenced each other and were unfamously infamous – there are stories …

file perch
clerk and

boss
peck at the stuff
laid out

before them
they hunt and peck
like giant chickens

in the office
we all

are giant chickens

where

 is the gravy?

Christler Chordoba

thees his the Christler Chordoba
look at hees lines
look how sinsual thay are
how natural it looks
and fiels a sleek smooth creature
its headlights wide
its grillwork devouring the air in front of the car
its tires pull the asphalt back consuming distance
as you sit in comfort almost relaxing
Chordoba   they can talk price   they can talk economy
but ees jus not the same as Chordoba

I am Recordo Montaban – and I like dese car
eet is to me what I want
jus run you han along it here see how it fiels
Chordoba
What a car   hat an ixperience in driving   Chordoba

Think of how you will fiel in it
how it will fiel in you
eemagin the rugged interior
the soothed hides and leathers of a great bull

touch the hood   fiel thee sleek lines of chrome
kees dee headlights   massage the tires
and grip firmly the bumper   AH!
Chordoba a word for grace   a word for elegance
its quiet simplicity so sure of itself with you
but eet is more than a car   eet iss a mood
that can only be understated
look how you move within it
look how it moves within you
Chordoba eet iss a car that you want
Chordoba a car that wants you

Chordoba is a fine compliment to a great house
like my hacienda in the hills where I vacation
eet iss a swift movement captured in the color of the sky
an essance
Chordoba the free spirit
Chordoba the subtle
Chordoba by Christler ees a new era of driving comfort
that unfolds with each turn of the road
with each moment of driving pleasure
Chordoba   YES
a truly great car

This was inspired by a TV commercial, as one might guess/

A Downtown Bank

the clock   exactly silent
above elevator doors; they are always
opening or
closing empty
the hall
carpet
looking new as ever
electrically swept
clock   monitors that I wave to, who knows?
schedules smooth
carpet
noiseless, waiting,
the clock wails
522 pee em
late and I am leaving
all this time timed
over the cafeteria tables
crowded   mum murmuring
of figures taking in figures
talking in figures figuring
out the curves   or a hip's swerve
noting the clock
timing is important and
so is the lounge where sleeping is allowed

an old man ... long memories
and the rose blush on his forehead
roses   roses in his dreams
giant roses cover the hills and fields
going on and on
his vision red with them for years
there is always that prayer
it lifts out of him   as breath by breath
he sits on the bench
wearing his proper gray hat set low for shade
a glow of afternoon sun   falls on him
a while longer   just a little while
it's so comfortable here ... he nods
all I want ... is my moment
by moment   the slowness dreaming

the birthday cake   the brand new bicycle
he rode all the way to the hills
his uncle smiling
had carried it into the house
wearing coveralls with wrenches in the pockets

all right   all right   asleep on the bench now
he holds the circles in his hands
knows what distance is

am I these hands?
bent joints   deep lines folding in the palms
fingers thick with arthritis
one summer   I felt they could breathe
strong ... he opens and   and closes them
withered flowers and leaves on the walk, dry
he asks, nodding to himself, slow
how long ... how long
is love

at the window   a guitar

one string   curled at the key

      outside   clouds move

Mother's Day ...

Mother, when you slip, I will still feel   you
And (know) this will never be through.

How I wish we'd confer   and warm comfit spread
As were we friends or lovers instead –

Of who we are.

It's said, Fate brings us all to be. That may be true
However, you cannot avoid the credits you're due.

As to the playwright so then to you for scenes in my life.
And your role so betaken that it's transferred to my wife.

Yet would I have you hover near, ever still
Until that day when I forfeit my will.

We'll enjoy that day and laugh instead
Of crying for losses, the illusory dead.

Celestials all we'll gather and sing a hearty round
And tell our tales with hindsight, fury, and sound.

The Food of the Gods will be our simple fare
At that Jubilee way up in the middle of the air.

This is another set of poems from about this period – also found in my notebooks. I include these for the same reasons I included the set of high school poems previously.

I remember Simas Kurdirka
The media turned and told me his story

Wanting the dreams of a fabled land, perhaps
Not the riches, gold, but worth
To follow convictions
Yet in the moments he could have been saved
The paper men made their long decision
He fell back into his world
So we know what we stand for

They Noticed

They noticed then
I noticed
How my attention wanders
Over paintings
Like
Snowflakes
In front of a window pane
The tiny jewelry of them
On wet velvet black
Rainbow crystals
To dream into
((Their))
Falling with
Piano note swirls
Or
Pausing
With halted air   to stare   white
Baby surprised
At me

I
Caught
My eyes
With
Her
Eyes
Black as the depths of an owl's
Searching
For prey
On a windy
Autumn
Night

Well,

    A cigarette

        Smashed out

    In the guacamole ...

        The morning ... after

****
Chapter Four

75/8 – 78/5   32nd Avenue

I continued writing, working part time, and learning the ropes of life, as it were. I crashed and burned my way through several relationships and so became risk avoidant for most all of this time. I have few photos from this period.

Where Eagles Dare, Open Mic

The poet writes, heedless
Of your opinion
With graphic reality – the words form on the page
Sketching a misty world
Which your mind
And then your soul make real – you are not alone
The poet fashions words into weapons
Scenery
Yet, do not be deceived
Even if the poem starts out
Whimsically
Or concerning the illusions of love
After all you are unprotected
Even naked
As you are drawn into the word
And strung along as the line is paid out
Whether it is through some detailed and novel tragedy,
Personal tribulation
Or humiliation
You tread along the path
Stepping where the poet's feet have dinted
Each phrase insists – leads on to the next
As your focus narrows
And looses sight of what is beyond the edge of the way
No matter how insane
You are married to the discourse and listen on
Your soul has been touched
And you go along for the ride
Abandon all hope
When enemies appear
And they strike you and cruelly
With blunt instruments
Scrambling away into an alleyway world
A dirty, howling, strung-out scabrous panhandler

A rapist, assaults you
A great red shaggy dog with foaming fangs
Growls and pants
As you run it unsteadily lopes along after you
From a saloon
An American cowboy in a white hat
Tosses you his six shooter
And you turn – take a shot
The hound's writhing death
Fills you with dread

Sudden laughter has you turn around
An emperor
In papier-mâché regalia
Is fearful of the rain
He implores you to apply lacquer to his bodice
Asks if you are a pedophile
If you will bathe
In the sacred fountain of blood
So as to wash away your sin sick soul
He asks about your graffiti tag
He hands you a laptop
And begs for forgiveness
As both of you squat
Relieving yourselves
In the sand at your feet

Finally, your poet finishes   you too
Are relieved
But there is no sand at your feet
Only a return
To the gift of silence
Which clears the palate
Before the next visionary journey   begins
And this is what happens   over and over
At an ordinary   open mic

Scars

1

Scars tell it like is   was
At one time
One moment of
Horror
When you
Become hidden   by what they still see of it
On you

Any wound   is real   a lesson
An instant that becomes
Years in the making – a book
Of sorrow
A choir of regrets
Singing in your bones
Rows of orderly memoirs have their cemetery echoes
Places where the scar hides   chime in

No matter how one prays   as one might
For release
There is none   from that which never
Knows   time

2

Out on the water
A sprinkling of rings
Insects … fish … some little thing

Leaves turning
Summer long gone   and
If you look close
You'll see them   at rest   there   amid

Fallen branches
Or underbrush
Clumps of torn up feathery parts
Through your frosty breath   and
The long silence   of chill air

Even the moon   has its marks
Even the sun   which makes our   colorful horizons
Wherein one's imagination may see it as you like it

Still   your scars   inform
Those who can read them

3

Not bruised nor broken
The night's hidden whimpering and mutters
The child violence
Left off   in the early morning hours
Without a mark
Without a sign
Questions that die   in the silence of what is not   ever   said

The   eyes   that say more
For what they've seen
For what they need
Of love
And all that they might dream for

at night somewhere in the
in a house near the sea
after her calm of knowing years
she still has an unreachable ideal
and he is afraid to reach
at night somewhere in the world
in a house near the sea
they are together
he reaches   holds her hand   says
that love is always incomplete
imperfect   each of them in their own way   loves now
they say this to each other's answers: "Yes, yes."
at night somewhere in the world
in a house near the sea
fog moves over the water
a ship sounds

Matches

in her living room
were kept on the coffee table
in a large glass bowl
shaped like a brandy snifter
for decoration   display or direction
it's full of matchbooks
from restaurants   shows
bars and resorts
the way she looks it up
is that it's all what she wants
to do
all that she wants inside
the vessel
are the matchbooks
laughingly juxtaposed
color pieces

I have matchbooks   placed here and there
some full   some half
some   just waiting   this one
on the mantle piece or   that one on the table
I play with them   striking
to set them ablaze
on soft afternoons
I watch their dreams move in the air

An Open Letter

So,
Here it is,
Finally,
A perfectly composed letter
From me –
To you.

You gave me life
And whisper therefore
Within these sparse lines.

How can I speak of this:
A small wonder, that
Years ago, some crying passion,
Has led, at long last, to this
Eventuality   this telling moment.

All these winters, springs, and summers
And I must say
That I've never told you
How I loved autumnal leaves,
About my favorite,
Catching fireflies and letting them go
Memory.

Or how, after his death,
I grew silent within the dreams I wove
And saw you watch me disappear.

We both knew the distance between words, glances,
And touch

And so, in that knowing, you
Were always close.
I did not know how to speak
Of the clear-silvered pool I'd found
Becalmed in its deliberate setting,
Secreted amid a misty forest,
Of how it expects my reflection,
And so calls me back
To drink its steeped solace.

There joy is as simple as fish surfacing,
Here and there,
To kiss rings of ripples
Soundless, deep, and free.

And freedom,
As birds fly, daring the cragged heights of age and wisdom,
So my heart too takes wing in all that sky
And with a sovereign's view
Of this lush dreaming valley.
I yearn …
I come down, soft as breath,
Near that pool on the other side,
Take rest,
And cast in all those troublesome stones.

in gutter water
some french-fries with their flowing
rainbow oil slicks

      despite what's said

           in the night's rain

      sleeping together,

           you turn, for comfort

                I hold you

                      without thought

Four billion years later I was

Waiting

At eighth and Irving

To catch a glimpse of you

The lover who

Had my dream lover's name

Who was, as my dream lover was

Patient

In the latitude and longitude

Of

Eighth and Irving

San Francisco

Gone

But at the same spot autumn

Sand holds out an arm to a warm shallow sea

Preventing Contact

but what he did was
play my guitar and sing
I mean to tell you that I was surprised
the way he loved the sound out of it

the first thing I thought
here he is
another one of Molly's bar hopping flings
I'd seen it before

he sat there across the table
blue jeans and plaid shirt
like some lumberjack hero
with well-traveled brown boots
and so much wind in his hair

his windswept features
the north wind
cold spirit
seemed barren
as the tundra

unlaughing
never warm
his voice deep
smoked
heated through the cold nights at a fire
or huddled under a bridge
I was afraid
of his romantic rambling
my self being settled

then
in the morning after
showing me to cook tortillas over an open flame
saying that he liked butter
as he spread it luxuriantly
the day he left
he spent time and talked freely
and
later
I found it
a fist sized sphere   dense metal
polished mirror bright   in memory
it is on the mantle piece
it draws the whole room in
as I touch it
my fingers curve away
bowing from themselves
preventing
contact

Yes! Give this book away!

When you give this book away, please initial it here, and indicate where and when you handed it off. I'd like these to meander the world over to perhaps migrate back to San Francisco as kind of message in a bottle. I look forward to its MUNI debut, seeing it on someone's bookshelf, or garage sale.

Initials   City   Date

_____

_____

_____

_____

_____

_____

_____

_____

_____

_____

Once this page is full, use any other page – go for it!

www.ingramcontent.com/pod-product-compliance
Lightning Source LLC
Chambersburg PA
CBHW032134040426
42449CB00005B/232